THEN AND
TOYS
THEN AND NOW

by Nadia Higgins

pogo

Ideas for Parents and Teachers

Pogo Books let children practice reading informational text while introducing them to nonfiction features such as headings, labels, sidebars, maps, and diagrams, as well as a table of contents, glossary, and index.

Carefully leveled text with a strong photo match offers early fluent readers the support they need to succeed.

Before Reading

• "Walk" through the book and point out the various nonfiction features. Ask the student what purpose each feature serves.

• Look at the glossary together. Read and discuss the words.

Read the Book

• Have the child read the book independently.

• Invite him or her to list questions that arise from reading.

After Reading

• Discuss the child's questions. Talk about how he or she might find answers to those questions.

• Prompt the child to think more. Ask: How are your toys like the toys in this book? How are they different? What is your favorite kind of toy?

Pogo Books are published by Jump!
5357 Penn Avenue South
Minneapolis, MN 55419
www.jumplibrary.com

Library of Congress Cataloging-in-Publication Data is available at www.loc.gov or upon request from the publisher.

ISBN: 978-1-64128-477-6 (hardcover)
ISBN: 978-1-64128-478-3 (paperback)
ISBN: 978-1-64128-479-0 (ebook)

Editor: Jenna Trnka
Designer: Molly Ballanger

Photo Credits: Rudmer Zwerver/Shutterstock, cover (left); Toxitz/Dreamstime, cover (right); Barry Lewis/Getty, 1 (left); Ivanastar/iStock, 1 (right); TheFarAwayKingdom/Shutterstock, 3; ClassicStock.com/SuperStock, 4; Image Source/iStock, 5; Doug Menuez/Forrester Images/Getty, 6-7; KenWiedermann/iStock, 8-9; Roland Kemp/Getty, 10; picture alliance/Getty, 11; M. Unal Ozmen/Shutterstock, 12-13 (background); domoremia/Getty, 12-13 (train set); JTBurrell/Getty, 12-13 (car); De Agostini Picture Library/Getty, 12-13 (airplane); John Bulmer/Getty, 14 (LEGOs); DieterMeyrl/iStock, 14 (robot); AlesiaKan/Shutterstock, 15; Ideabug/iStock, 16-17; True Images/Alamy, 17; Kansas City Star/Getty, 18-19; LightField Studios/Shutterstock, 20-21; Tony Stock/Shutterstock, 23.

Printed in the United States of America at Corporate Graphics in North Mankato, Minnesota.

TABLE OF CONTENTS

CHAPTER 1
Simple Toys..................................4

CHAPTER 2
New Features..............................10

CHAPTER 3
Fads and Favorites 14

ACTIVITIES & TOOLS
Try This!....................................22
Glossary....................................23
Index..24
To Learn More..........................24

CHAPTER 1

....

SIMPLE TOYS

hula hoop ·····▶

Toys help us play. Pretend. Think. Some even help us move. The hula hoop was a huge **fad** in the 1950s.

Hula hoops are still toys today. But they look different. How have toys changed over time?

Toys in the 1700s were very simple. Spinning tops. Kites. Balls made from leather. They were made by hand. With what? Things found in nature. Corn husk dolls were popular.

corn husk
doll

By the late 1800s, kids played with toys to learn, too. Puzzles. Board games. Letter blocks for spelling. These were made of wood, metal, glass, or rubber. Toys are still made from these materials. But now they are **manufactured** in factories.

TAKE A LOOK!

Puzzles are toys we have to **solve**. Take a look at these different puzzles. How have they changed?

PIGS IN CLOVER
Players try to get the balls through the maze.

RUBIK'S CUBE
Players rotate the sides of the cube to try to get all same-colored squares on the same side.

JIGSAW PUZZLE
Players fit cut pieces together to form a picture.

PERPLEXUS
Players rotate a clear ball to try to get a smaller ball inside through a maze of plastic twists and turns.

CHAPTER 2

NEW FEATURES

In 1902, the teddy bear was invented. This toy was soft and cute. You could move its arms and legs.

Today, stuffed animals have more features. Some speak. Some have **sensors** to sense movement. Many can move on their own.

By the 1920s, new kinds of **transportation** were everywhere. Toy trains, cars, trucks, and planes became popular. These new toys looked like the real thing. They had spinning wheels and parts. **Electric** trains sped around a toy track.

CHAPTER 3

FADS AND FAVORITES

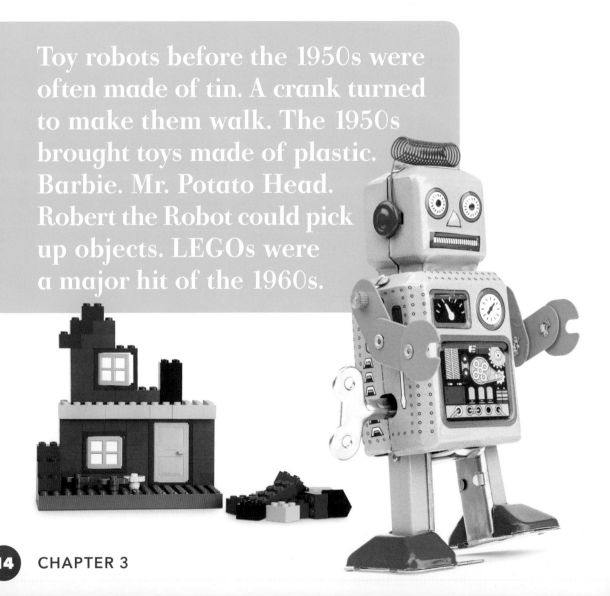

Toy robots before the 1950s were often made of tin. A crank turned to make them walk. The 1950s brought toys made of plastic. Barbie. Mr. Potato Head. Robert the Robot could pick up objects. LEGOs were a major hit of the 1960s.

People were amazed by LEGOs. Imagine if they saw LEGOs today. Now you can **program** a LEGO robot!

In the 1970s, toys started reflecting what was on-screen. Kids spent hours playing with their favorite action figures. What were the characters from? Star Wars. Sesame Street. Disney. More toys used batteries. High-tech toys lit up. They had fun sound effects.

Almost all dolls used to have white skin. That has changed over time. In the 1990s, girls could create an American Girl look-alike doll. She could pick the doll's hair, eye, and skin color to match her own.

virtual reality
goggles

Now, Wi-Fi, sensors, and computer chips make toys smarter. Toy cars can take video. **Virtual reality** goggles make you feel like you are somewhere else. What do you think toys of the future will be able to do?

DID YOU KNOW?

Toy stores used to label some toys for girls and some for boys. Not anymore. Major toy stores are dropping those signs. They want boys and girls to shop for any toy they want.

ACTIVITIES & TOOLS

MAKE A JIGSAW PUZZLE

Use your own artwork or favorite picture to make a jigsaw puzzle!

What You Need:

- a drawing or picture
- cardboard that is larger than your picture
- a large, heavy book
- glue
- pencil
- scissors

❶ Glue your drawing or picture to the cardboard. Make sure it is smooth, with no bubbles or wrinkles.

❷ Set the big, heavy book on the picture as it dries. Once the glue is completely dry, trim off the cardboard edges that are sticking out.

❸ Turn the picture over. On the back, draw the puzzle shapes you will cut out. It works better if the pieces are not too small or fancy.

❹ Cut along the lines you drew to cut out your puzzle pieces.

❺ Mix up the pieces up. How long does it take you to put your jigsaw puzzle together?

GLOSSARY

electric: Operated by electricity.

fad: Something that is very popular for a short time.

manufactured: Made from raw materials by hands or machines.

program: To give a machine instructions to make it work in a certain way.

sensors: Instruments that can pick up changes, such as sound, touch, or light, and transmit the information to a controlling device.

solve: To find a solution, explanation, or answer.

transportation: A means of moving people or things from one place to another.

virtual reality: An artificial environment that is experienced through senses, such as sights and sounds, and is created by computers to feel as real as possible.

INDEX

action figures 17

balls 6, 9

Barbie 14, 18

batteries 17

board games 8

corn husk dolls 6

dolls 6, 18

fad 4

hula hoop 4, 5

kites 6

LEGOs 14, 15

letter blocks 8

Mr. Potato Head 14

puzzles 8, 9

robots 14, 15

sensors 11, 21

Snow Snake 6

sound effects 17

spinning tops 6

stuffed animals 11

teddy bear 10

transportation toys 12

virtual reality goggles 21

Wi-Fi 21

TO LEARN MORE

Finding more information is as easy as 1, 2, 3.

❶ Go to www.factsurfer.com

❷ Enter "toysthenandnow" into the search box.

❸ Click the "Surf" button to see a list of websites.

FACT SURFER